Seal

Meredith Hooper

Illustrated by Bert Kitchen

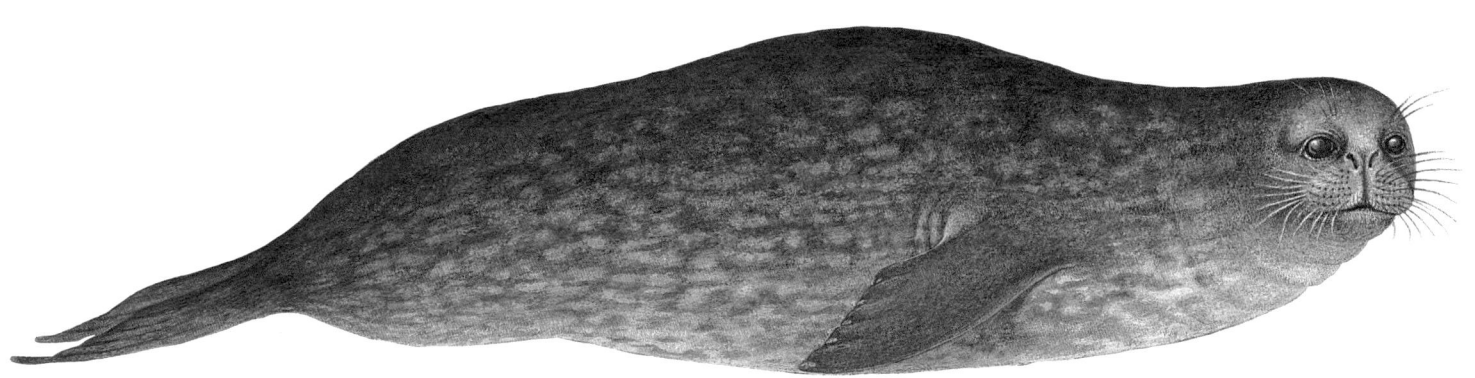

This book is about Weddell seals in the Antarctic.

CAMBRIDGE
UNIVERSITY PRESS

The seal is on the ice.

Seals move very slowly on the ice. They flop along,
heaving their big, heavy bodies.

She goes into the water through a hole in the ice.

Seals are warm-blooded, like us. They must keep warm.
Their skin is covered with thick, bristly hair. Under their skin
they have a thick layer of fat called blubber. The hair and the
blubber keep the seals warm.

The seal swims fast.

Seals can swim quickly because their smooth, sleek shape moves easily through the water. Seals can turn, dive and roll. They use their flippers like paddles.

The seals make a lot of noise under water. They call to each other in hoots, clicks and whistles. Up on the ice, seals just snore.

She dives down deep into the sea.

 Just under the ice, the water is a beautiful blue-green colour.
But deep down, where the light cannot reach, the water is dark.
Seals have big eyes to help them to see under water.

The seal is hunting squid. Squid swim fast, but the seal swims faster.

 There is no food for seals up on the ice. All their food is in the sea. Weddell seals eat mostly fish and some squid.

She is a long way down under the ice.

Weddell seals dive deeper than most other seals.
Their favourite fish can be 500 metres down, near
the bottom of the sea.

The seal swims up. She is looking for the hole in the ice.

Seals must breathe air. The hole in the ice is the seal's breathing-hole.

She pokes her head out of the hole and takes a deep breath.

Weddell seals can stay under water longer than many other seals. They can stay under water without breathing for up to 90 minutes, but they usually stay under for about 17 minutes.

9

The seal looks around.

 In the spring, mother seals give birth to their pups on the ice. The pups have long, grey fur and a thin layer of blubber to keep them warm. They make a sound like lambs bleating.

Her pup is waiting.

Young seals do not eat fish and squid. They drink warm, rich milk from their mothers. The young seals grow very quickly.

11

The mother seal and her pup lie on the ice.

A small group of mother seals and their pups stay together all summer.
The seals stay near the breathing-hole. They sleep in the sunshine.
Although it is summer, it is still very cold.

The mother seal takes her pup to the breathing-hole for a swim.

Young seals try their first swim when they are less than two weeks old. The mother seals slide into the water and the pups follow. After four weeks, the young seals can dive and catch fish with their mothers.

The male seal spends most of his time in the water. He guards the breathing-hole for the group of mothers and their pups.

When winter comes, terrible storms blow across the ice.

When blizzards blow across the ice, the temperature
can drop to minus 50 degrees Celsius (– 50 °C).

The seals stay in the water all winter.

The water is calm and not nearly as cold as the air above the ice.
   In winter, the ice is very thick but the seals still have to keep their breathing-hole open. They do this by biting and scraping at the ice with their teeth.

South Pole

The huge continent of Antarctica spreads across the southernmost part of the world.
It is covered in ice and snow.

The South Pole is far inland. Below the South Pole there are 90 metres of snow. Below the snow there are 2,650 metres of ice.

Below the ice is the rock of the continent.

Weddell seals live around the coast of Antarctica and the nearby islands. Weddell seals can only be seen in the Antarctic because they cannot live in captivity.